a Book for the Bog

JOKES FOR THE JOHN

Managing Editor: Simon Melhuish
Series Editor: Nikole G Bamford
Research: Gavin Webster
Design and Illustrations: Gary Sherwood

Designed and compiled by
Mad Moose Press
for
Lagoon Books
PO Box 311, KT2 5QW, UK
PO Box 990676, Boston, MA 02199, USA

ISBN: 1-904139-33-7

www.madmoosepress.com
www.lagoongames.com

Printed in China

a Book for the Bog

JOKES FOR THE JOHN

Why do psychiatrists give patients shock treatment?
To prepare them for the bill.

◊

What's the best way to make sure you always remember your
wife's birthday?
Forget it once.

◊

What's the difference between marriage
and divorce?
Marriage is grand, divorce is about ten grand.

◊

Why do women live longer than men?
Someone has to stay around to clean up after them.

◊

What's the difference between a good lawyer and
a great lawyer?
A good lawyer knows the law, a great lawyer knows the judge.

◊

Why didn't the hen-pecked husband speak to his wife for
a month?
He didn't want to interrupt her.

◊

What's the disadvantage of keeping an open mind?
Your ideas might fall out.

◊

How do you get a man to do sit-ups?
Put the TV remote control between his toes.

When does a woman care deeply for her husband's company?
When he owns it.

♦

Why does history keep repeating itself?
Because we weren't listening the first time.

♦

Why did the cannibal policeman get the sack?
He was caught grilling his suspects.

♦

What's the best way to get a youthful figure?
Ask a woman her age.

♦

What do you call a man with a car on his head?
Jack.

♦

How many gorillas does it take to screw in a light bulb?
Only one, but it gets through a lot of light bulbs!

♦

What do you know if you see a man opening a car door for his wife?
That the car or the wife is new.

♦

Why do hummingbirds hum?
Because they don't know the words.

♦

What did the fish say when it hit a concrete wall?
"Dam!"

A woman accompanied her husband to the doctor's office. After his check-up, the doctor called the wife into his office alone. He said, "Your husband is suffering from a very severe disease, combined with horrible stress. If you don't do the following, your husband will surely die. Each morning, fix him a healthy breakfast. Be pleasant, and make sure he is in a good mood. For lunch make him a nutritious meal. For dinner prepare an especially nice meal for him. Don't burden him with chores, as he probably had a hard day. Don't discuss your problems with him — it will only make his stress worse. If you can do this for the next 10 months to a year, I think your husband will regain his health completely."

On the way home, the husband asked his wife, "What did the doctor say?"

"You're going to die," she replied.

A man goes to the doctor and says, "Doctor I don't know whether I'm a wigwam or a tepee."

To which the doctor replies, "You are obviously two tents."

I walked into a bar the other day and ordered a double. The bartender brought out a guy who looked just like me.

In the first year of marriage the man speaks and the woman listens. In the second year of marriage the woman speaks and the man listens. After that, they both speak and the neighbors listen.

They say when a man holds a woman's hand before marriage, it is love; after marriage, it is self-defense.

♦

Little Johnny was caught swearing by his teacher.
"Johnny," she said, "you shouldn't use that kind of language. Where did you hear such talk, anyway?"
"My daddy said it," he responded.
"Well, that doesn't matter," explained the teacher. "You don't even know what it means."
"I do, too!" Little Johnny retorted. "It means the car won't start."

♦

Two fleas come out of the cinema to find that it's raining hard. One flea turns to the other and says, "Do you want to walk or wait for a dog?"

Two lawyers are in a bank when a gang of armed robbers bursts in. While several of the robbers take the money from the tellers, others line the customers, including the lawyers, up against a wall, and proceed to take their wallets, watches, etc. While this is going on lawyer number one jams something into lawyer number two's hand.

Without looking down, lawyer number two whispers, "What is this?"

Lawyer number one replies, "It's that money I owe you."

On a rural road a policeman pulled a farmer over and said: "Sir, do you realize your wife fell out of the car several miles back?"

To which the farmer replied, "Thank God, I thought I had gone deaf!"

A hillbilly was traveling across Texas when a state policeman pulled him over.

"You got any I.D.?" the patrolman asked.

"'Bout what?" the hillbilly replied.

A woman has the last word in any argument. Anything a man says after that is the beginning of a new argument.

Committee: A group of people that keeps minutes and wastes hours.

An encyclopedia salesman knocks on a door and it's opened by a 12-year-old boy holding a glass of Scotch and smoking a cigar.

"Is your mother in?" asks the salesman.

The boy taps some ash onto the carpet and says, "What do you think?"

○

A man walks into a bar swinging a set of jumper leads above his head. The barman looks over and says, "You're not going to start anything in here!"

○

All the toilet seats at the police station have been stolen. The thief is still at large, and the police have nothing to go on.

○

Psychiatrist: What's your problem?
Patient: I think I'm a chicken.
Psychiatrist: How long has this been going on?
Patient: Ever since I was an egg!

○

My therapist told me the way to achieve true inner peace is to finish what I start. So far today, I have finished two bags of chips and a chocolate cake. I feel better already.

○

Innkeeper: The room is $15 per night or it's $5 if you make your own bed.
Guest: I'll make my own bed.
Innkeeper: Good. I'll get you some wood.

How many psychologists does it take to change a light bulb?
None, the bulb will change itself when it is ready.

❍

What's green, and if it fell out of a tree, would kill you?
A pool table.

❍

What's brown and runs round the garden?
A fence.

❍

When do cannibals leave the table?
When everyone's eaten.

❍

Why was the unsuccessful boxer known as 'Picasso'?
He was always on the canvas.

❍

What do you call cattle with a sense of humor?
Laughing stock.

❍

How do you confuse a blonde?
You don't. They're born that way.

❍

Why is Christmas just like a day at the office?
You do all the work and the fat bloke with the suit gets
all the credit.

❍

How do you catch a squirrel?
Climb a tree and act like a nut.

How many mystery writers does it take to screw in a light bulb?
Two: one to screw it almost all the way in and the other to give
it a surprising twist at the end.

What do you call Santa's helpers?
Subordinate Clauses.

What do you see when you look into a blonde's eyes?
The back of her head.

How do you know when you're really getting old?
The candles cost more than the cake.

How do blonde brain cells die?
Alone.

Why did the man keep his wife under the bed?
He thought she was a little potty.

One day, Bill and Tom went to a restaurant for dinner. As soon as the waiter brought out two steaks, Bill quickly picked out the bigger steak for himself.

Tom wasn't happy about that: When are you going to learn to be polite?

Bill: If you had the chance to pick first, which one would you pick?

Tom: The smaller piece, of course.

Bill: What are you whining about then? The smaller piece is what you want, right?

🌢

Jack was living in Arizona during a heat wave when the following took place.

"It's just too hot to wear clothes today," complained Jack as he stepped out of the shower. "Honey, what would the neighbors think if I mowed the lawn like this?"

"Probably that I married you for your money."

🌢

A man walks into a butcher's shop and inquires of the butcher, "Are you a gambling man?"

The butcher says he is, so the man said, "I bet you $50 that you can't reach up and touch that meat hanging on the hooks up there."

The butcher says "I'm not betting on that."

"But I thought you were a gambling man," the man retorts.

"Well, I am" says the butcher, "but the steaks are too high."

Knock! Knock!
Who's there?
Harry.
Harry who?
Harry up and let me in!

A man walked into a bar and asked who the Great Dane outside belonged to. A hulking figure covered in scars and tattoos at the end of the bar growled: "He's mine. Why?"
"Er, my dog just killed him," replied the man nervously.
"What?" roared the hulking figure, "That's impossible. That dog weighs more than I do. And he's more dangerous. I've seen him kill three grizzlies at the same time."
"Well," says the man, "He choked on my Chihuahua."

A new teacher was trying to make use of her psychology courses. She started her class by saying, "Everyone who thinks you're stupid, stand up!"
After a few seconds, Little Johnny stood up. The teacher said, "Do you think you're stupid, Little Johnny?"
"No, ma'am, but I hate to see you standing there all by yourself!"

Marriage means commitment. Of course, so does insanity.

Three strings walk into a bar. The bartender throws them out, yelling "Can't you read the sign?! I don't serve strings." The strings try again, and again the bartender kicks them out. Finally, one of the strings gets the idea to mess himself up a little. He walks into the bar. The bartender scowls, "What's wrong with you? Can't you read? I don't serve strings!" The string replies, "I'm a frayed knot!"

♦

There was an inebriated driver who was pulled up by the police. When the policeman opened the door, the driver fell out.
"YOU'RE DRUNK!" exclaimed the police officer.
"Thank God for that!" said the drunk, "I thought the steering had gone."

♦

Woman to policeman: Help! Help! My husband's been fighting for half an hour.
Policeman: Why didn't you call us before?
Woman: He was winning up to a minute ago.

♦

A boat carrying red paint and a boat carrying blue paint crashed into each other.
Apparently, the crew were marooned.

♦

Young Son: I heard that in some parts of the world a man doesn't know his wife until he marries her. Is it true, Dad?
Dad: That happens in every country, son.

A hole has appeared in the ladies' changing rooms at the sports club.
Police are looking into it.

◐

Two vampire bats wake up in the middle of the night, thirsty for blood. One says, "Let's fly out of the cave and get a bite to eat."
"We're new here," says the second one. "It's dark out, and we don't know where to look. We'd better wait until the other bats go with us."
The first bat replies, "Who needs them? I can find some blood somewhere." He flies out of the cave.
When he returns, he is covered in blood.
The second bat says excitedly, "Where did you get the blood?"
The first bat takes his friend to the mouth of the cave. Pointing into the night, he asks, "See that black cliff over there?"
"Yes," the other bat answers.
"Well," says the first bat, "I didn't."

This guy dies and is sent down to Hell. Satan meets him and shows him the doors to three rooms and says he must choose one of the rooms to spend eternity in. Satan opens the first door. In the room there are people standing in cow manure up to their necks. The man says "No, please show me the next room."

Satan shows him the next room and this one contains people with cow manure up to their noses. And so the man says no again. Finally, Satan shows him the third and final room. This time there are people in there with cow manure up to their knees drinking cups of tea and eating cakes.

So the bloke says, "I'll choose this room," and in he goes. Ten minutes later he's standing there eating his cake and drinking his tea thinking, "Well, it could be worse," when the door opens. Satan pops his head around, and says, "Right. Tea-break is over. Back on your heads!"

◐

A young husband with an inferiority complex insisted he was just a little pebble on a vast beach. The marriage counselor, trying to be creative, told him, "If you want to save your marriage, you'd better be a little boulder."

◐

A friend got some vinegar in his ear, now he suffers from pickled hearing.

◐

Sign in restaurant window: Eat now — Pay waiter.

A man yells to his wife, "Pack your bags. I've won the lottery!"
The wife excitedly asks, "Should I pack clothes for cold or warm weather?"
He says, "Pack 'em all, you're leaving!"

Two cannibals sat beside a large fire, after eating the best meal they'd had in ages.
"Your wife sure makes a good roast," commented the first cannibal.
"Yeah," replied the second. "I'm really going to miss her..."

A policeman spots a little old lady driving and knitting at the same time. Driving up beside he, he shouts out the window, "Pull over!"
"No," she shouts back, "A pair of socks!"

A young woman went into a bank to withdraw some money. "Can you identify yourself?" asked the bank clerk. The young woman opened her handbag, took out a mirror, looked into it and said, "Yes, it's me all right."

The bride, upon her engagement, went to her mother to give her the good news. "I've found a man just like Father!" she gushed.
Her mother replied, "So what do you want from me, sympathy?"

A New York City stockbroker moved to the country and bought a piece of land. He went to the local feed and livestock store and talked to the proprietor about how he was going to take up chicken farming. He then asked to buy 100 chicks.

"That's a lot of chicks," commented the proprietor.

"I mean business," the city slicker replied.

A week later he was back again. "I need another 100 chicks," he said.

"Boy, you are serious about this chicken farming," the man told him.

"Yeah," the broker replied. "If I can iron out a few problems."

"Problems?" asked the proprietor.

"Yeah," replied the New Yorker, "I think I planted that last batch too close together."

A man is driving down a country road, when he spots a farmer standing in the middle of a huge field of grass. He pulls the car over to the side of the road and notices that the farmer is just standing there, doing nothing, looking at nothing. The man gets out of the car, walks all the way out to the farmer and asks him, "Ah excuse me, but what are you doing?"

The farmer replies, "I'm trying to win a Nobel Prize."

"How?" asks the man, puzzled.

"Well, I heard they give the Nobel Prize to people who are out standing in their field."

A man was painting his house, when a beggar approached asking if he could earn a few bucks. The man thought about it for a minute, and said, "Take a can of this paint, go around to the back of the house, and paint my porch."

An hour later the beggar returned, saying he was finished. Surprised, the man said, "Already?"

"Yes," the beggar said, "but it wasn't a Porsche, it was a Mercedes!"

A man walks into a doctor's office. He has a cucumber up his nose, a carrot in his left ear and a banana in his right ear.

"What's the matter with me?" he asks the doctor.

The doctor replies, "You're not eating properly."

A serious drunk walked into a bar and, after staring for some time at the only woman seated at the bar, walked over to her and kissed her. She jumped up and slapped him silly.

He immediately apologized and explained, "I'm sorry. I thought you were my wife. You look exactly like her."

"Why, you worthless, insufferable, wretched, no good drunk!" she screamed.

"Funny," he muttered, "you even sound exactly like her."

A clergyman walking down a country lane sees a young farmer struggling to right an overturned cart.

"You look hot, my son," said the cleric. "Why don't you rest a moment, and then I'll give you a hand."

"No thanks," said the young man. "My father wouldn't like it."

"Don't be silly," the minister said. "Everyone is entitled to a break. Come and have a drink of water."

Again the young man protested that his father would be upset.

Losing his patience, the clergyman said, "Your father must be a real slave driver. Tell me where I can find him and I'll give him a piece of my mind!"

"Well," replied the young farmer, "he's under the cart."

Two cannibals are eating a clown. One says to the other, "Does this taste funny to you?"

The devil visited a lawyer's office and made him an offer. "I can arrange some things for you," the devil said. "I'll increase your income five-fold. Your partners will love you; your clients will respect you; you'll have four months of vacation each year and live to be a 100. All I require in return is that your wife's soul, your children's souls, and their children's souls rot in hell for eternity."

The lawyer thought for a moment. "What's the catch?" he asked.

A policeman was interrogating a very intoxicated man who was bleeding profusely from numerous cuts all over his face and body. The officer asked, "Can you describe the person who did this to you?"

The man replied, "That's what I was doing when he hit me."

A customer was bothering the waiter in a restaurant. First, he asked that the air conditioning be turned up because he was too hot, then he asked it be turned down because he was too cold, and so on for about half an hour.

Surprisingly, the waiter was very patient, he walked back and forth and never once got angry. Finally a second customer asked him why he didn't throw out the pest.

"Oh, I really don't care or mind," said the waiter with a smile. "We don't even have an air conditioner."

A horse walks into a bar and the barman says...
"Why the long face?"

🌢

Little Johnny was talking to a couple of boys in the schoolyard.
Each was bragging about how great their fathers are. The first
one said: "Well, my father runs the fastest. He can fire an arrow,
and start to run — I tell you, he gets there before the arrow!"
The second one said: "Ha! You think that's fast! My father is a
hunter. He can shoot his gun and be there before the bullet!"
Little Johnny listened to the other two boys and shook his head.
He then said, "You two know nothing about fast. My father is a
civil servant. He finishes work at 4:30 and he's always
home by 3:45!"

🌢

Two robbers were robbing a hotel. The first one said, "I hear
sirens. Jump!"
The second one said, "But we're on the 13th floor!"
The first one screamed back, "This is no time to be
superstitious."

🌢

Knock! Knock!
Who's there?
Atch.
Atch who?
Bless you.

🌢

How careers end...
Lawyers are disbarred.
Ministers are defrocked.
Electricians are delighted.

Walking up to a department store's fabric counter, a pretty girl asked: "I want to buy this material for a dress. How much does it cost?"

"Only one kiss per yard" replied the smirking male clerk.

"That's fine," replied the girl. "I'll take ten yards."

With anticipation written all over his face, the clerk quickly measured out and wrapped the cloth, then teasingly held it out.

The girl snapped up the package and pointed to a little old man standing beside her. "Grandpa will pay the bill," she smiled.

A man was standing at a bus stop eating french fries when he was joined by an old lady with her dog. The dog was watching the man hungrily and after a while began to whine and paw at his legs. "Do you mind if I throw him a bit?" the man asked the old lady.

"Not at all," she replied.

With that the man picked up the dog and threw him over a wall.

Two cowboys come upon an Indian lying on his stomach with his ear to the ground. One of the cowboys stops and says to the other, "You see that Indian?"

"Yeah," says the other cowboy.

"Look," says the first one, "he's listening to the ground. He can hear things for miles in any direction."

Just then the Indian looks up. "Covered wagon," he says, "about two miles away. Two horses, one brown, one white. Man, woman, child, household effects in wagon."

"Incredible!" says the cowboy to his friend. "This Indian knows how far away they are, how many horses, what color they are, who is in the wagon, and what is in the wagon. Amazing!"

The Indian looks up and says, "Ran over me about a half hour ago."

A 92-year-old man went to the doctor in New Orleans to get a physical. A few days later, the doctor saw the man walking down the street with a gorgeous young lady on his arm. At his follow-up visit, the doctor said to the man, "You're really doing great, aren't you?"

The man replied, "Just doing what you said, Doctor: 'Get a hot mamma and be cheerful.'"

The Doctor said, "I didn't say that. I said you've got a heart murmur. Be careful!"

A blind man with a guide dog at his side walks into a shop. He picks the dog up by the tail, and starts swinging it around in circles over his head.

The manager comes over and asks if he can be of assistance. The blind man says, "No thanks. I'm just looking."

Little Johnny's kindergarten class was on a field trip to their local police station where they saw pictures of the 10 most wanted men tacked to a bulletin board. One of the youngsters pointed to a picture and asked if it really was the photo of a wanted person. "Yes," said the policeman. "The detectives want him very badly."

So Little Johnny asked, "Why didn't you keep him when you took his picture?"

●

At a local coffee bar, a young woman was expounding on her idea of the perfect mate to some of her friends.

"The man I marry must be a shining light amongst company. He must be musical. Tell jokes. Sing. And stay home at night!"

An old granny overheard and spoke up, "If that's all you want, dear, get a TV!"

●

A man was walking along the beach one day and came across a lamp. He picked it up, rubbed it, and a genie popped out.
The genie told him he would grant him three wishes.
"First," the guy began, "I'd like a million dollars."
POOF! A million dollars was suddenly showing on his checkbook balance.
"Second," he continued, "I'd like a brand new Rolls Royce."
POOF! A Rolls Royce appeared right in front of him.
"Third," the bloke smirked, "I'd like to be irresistible to women."
POOF! He turned into a box of chocolates.

●

Overweight is something that just sort of snacks up on you.

A man's car stalled on a country road one morning. When the man got out to fix it, a cow came along and stopped beside him. "Your trouble is probably in the carburetor," said the cow. Startled, the man jumped back and ran down the road until he met a farmer. The amazed man told the farmer his story.

"Was it a large red cow with a brown spot over the right eye?" asked the farmer.

"Yes, yes," the man replied.

"Oh! that'd be Bessie," said the farmer. "Pay no attention. She doesn't know a thing about cars."

A little old lady goes into a shop and explains to the assistant that she wants some wool to knit a coat for her dog. "How much do you want?" asks the assistant.

"I don't know," says the little old lady.

"Why don't you bring your dog in and then we can measure him?" suggests the assistant.

"Oh no, I couldn't do that," says the old lady. "It's meant to be a surprise for his birthday."

A woman's husband had been slipping in and out of a coma for several months, yet she had stayed by his bedside every day. One day, when he came to, he motioned her to come nearer. He whispered, eyes full of tears, "You know what? You have been with me all through the bad times. When I got fired, you were there. When my business failed, you were there. When I got shot, you were by my side. When our house burnt down, you were there. When my health started failing, you were by my side. You know what?"

"What dear?" she gently asked.

"I think you are bad luck," he said.

The last argument was my fault. My wife asked, "What's on the TV?"
I said, "Dust!"

A man went to visit a friend and was amazed to find him playing chess with his dog. He watched the game in astonishment for a while. "I can hardly believe my eyes!" he exclaimed. "That's the cleverest dog I've ever seen."
"Nah, he's not so smart," the friend replied. "I've beaten him three games out of five."

The Smiths were going camping in France. As they sat in the queue to board the ferry Mrs. Smith suddenly said, "I wish we'd brought the kitchen table."

"We've already packed too much" said her husband looking round at the pile of luggage in the back of the car.

"I know," said Mrs. Smith, "But the ferry tickets are on the kitchen table."

A drunken man gets on the bus late one night, staggers up the aisle, and sits next to an elderly woman. She looks the man up and down and says, "I've got news for you. You're going straight to hell!"

The man jumps up out of his seat and shouts, "Man, I'm on the wrong bus!"

Little Johnny was practicing the violin in the living room while his father was trying to read in the den. The family dog was lying in the den, and as the screeching sounds of Little Johnny's violin reached his ears, he began to howl loudly.

The father listened to the dog and the violin as long as he could. Then he jumped up, slammed his paper to the floor and yelled above the noise, "For pity's sake, can't you play something the dog doesn't know?"

They say man is incomplete until he is married. Then he is truly finished.

A child comes home from his first day at school. His mother asks, "Well, what did you learn today?"
The kid replies, "Not enough. They want me to come back tomorrow."

Graduates with a science degree ask: Why does it work?
Graduates with an engineering degree ask: How does it work?
Graduates with an accounting degree ask: How much will it cost?
Graduate with an arts degree ask: Do you want fries with that?

Five-year-old Little Johnny was lost, so he went up to a policeman and said, "I've lost my dad!"
The policeman asked, "What's he like?"
Little Johnny replied, "Beer and women!"

A couple of idiots in a pickup truck drove into a timber merchants. One of the idiots entered the office and said, "We need some four-by-twos."
The clerk said, "You mean two-by-fours, don't you?"
The idiot said, "I'll go check," and went back to the truck. He returned a minute later and said, "Yeah, I meant two-by-fours."
"All right. How long do you need them?"
The customer paused for a minute and said, "I'd better go check." After a while, he returned to the office and said, "A long time. We're gonna build a house."

Three dead bodies turn up at the mortuary, all with very big smiles on their faces. The Coroner calls the police to show them what's happened. A Detective Inspector is sent and is taken straight to the first body.

"Bob Smith, 60, died of heart failure while with his girlfriend. That explains the enormous smile, Inspector," says the coroner.

The Inspector is taken to the second dead man. "Jim Brady, 25, won $50,000 on the lottery, spent it all on whiskey and drank himself to death, hence the smile."

"Nothing unusual here," thinks the Inspector, and asks to be shown the last body.

"Ah," says the Coroner, "this is the most unusual one. Craig Jackson, 30, struck by lightning."

"Why is he smiling, then?" inquires the Inspector.

To which the coroner replies, "He thought he was having his picture taken."

🜂

A man walks into a bar and yells "Bartender, give me twenty shots of your best single malt Scotch!"

The bartender pours the shots and the man drinks them down one at a time, as fast as he can.

The bartender says "Wow, I never saw anybody drink that fast."

The man replies, "Well, you'd drink fast if you had what I have."

The bartender says, "Oh my God, what do you have?"

The man says, "Fifty-seven cents."

Knock! Knock!
Who's there?
Isabel.
Isabel who?
Isabel broken? I had to knock.

◐

The four food groups: Fast, Frozen, Instant, and Chocolate.

◐

An aged farmer and his wife were leaning against the edge of their pig-pen when the old woman wistfully recalled that the next week would mark their golden wedding anniversary. "Let's have a party, Homer," she suggested. "Let's kill a pig." The farmer scratched his grizzled head. "Gee, Ethel," he finally answered, "I don't see why the pig should take the blame for something that happened fifty years ago."

Three old ladies are sitting in a diner, chatting about various things. One lady says, "You know, I'm getting really forgetful. This morning, I was standing at the top of the stairs, and I couldn't remember whether I had just come up or was about to go down."

The second lady says, "You think that's bad? The other day, I was sitting on the edge of my bed, and I couldn't remember whether I was going to bed or had just woken up!"

The third lady smiles smugly. "Well, my memory's just as good as it's always been, touch wood."

She raps the table. With a startled look on her face, she asks, "Who's there?"

♦

The nurse next door has changed her name to Appendix. She's hoping one of the surgeons will take her out.

♦

A man goes to a dermatologist with a rare skin disease. The doctor says, "Try a milk bath." So the man goes to a shop and asks for enough milk to take a bath. The shop owner asks, "Do you want that pasteurized?"

"Nah," the man replied. "Up to my chin should do it."

♦

Men are like fine wine. They all start out like grapes, and it's a woman's job to stomp on them and keep them in the dark until they mature into something you'd like to have dinner with.

A soldier who lost his rifle was reprimanded by his captain and was told he would have to pay for it.

"Sir," gulped the soldier. "Suppose I lost a tank. Surely I would not have to pay for that?"

"Yes you would, too!" bellowed the captain. "Even if it took the rest of your life."

"Well," said the soldier, "now I know why the captain goes down with his ship."

When a man's printer type began to grow faint, he called a local repair shop where a friendly man informed him that the printer probably needed only to be cleaned. Because the shop charged $30 for such cleanings, he told him he might be better off reading the printer's manual and trying the job himself.

Pleasantly surprised by his candor, the man asked, "Does your boss know that you discourage business?"

"Actually, it's my boss's idea," the employee replied sheepishly. "We usually make more money on repairs if we let people try to fix things themselves first."

After the church service, a little boy told the pastor, "When I grow up, I'm going to give you some money."

"Well, thank you," replied the pastor, "but why?"

"Because my daddy says you're one of the poorest preachers we've ever had."

What did the neurotic pig say to the farmer?
You take me for grunted.

♦

What do you get when you cross a librarian with a lawyer?
All the information you need, but you can't understand a word
of it.

♦

What do Eskimos get from sitting on the ice too long?
Polaroids.

♦

What do you get when you cross the Godfather with a lawyer?
An offer you can't understand.

♦

How many civil servants does it take to change a light bulb?
45: one to change the bulb, and 44 to do the paperwork.

♦

Why do monks always wear brown?
It's just their habit.

♦

How do you kill a circus?
Go for the juggler.

♦

What's gray, has four legs and a trunk?
A mouse going on holiday.

How many nuclear engineers does it take to change
a light bulb?
Seven. One to install the new bulb and six to work out what to
do with the old one for the next 10,000 years.

What do you get when you cross a dyslexic agnostic with
an insomniac?
Someone who lies awake at night wondering whether there
is a dog.

How do you change a blonde's mind?
Blow in her ear.

Why do cows wear bells?
Because their horns don't work.

Did you hear about the two fat athletes?
One ran in short bursts and the other in burst shorts.

As Judy was driving down the motorway, her car phone rang. Answering, she heard her husband Bob's voice urgently warning her, "Judy, I just heard on the news that there's a car going the wrong way on the motorway. Please be careful!" "It's much worse than that!" said Judy. "It's not just one car. It's hundreds of them!"

⬤

A drunk was in front of a judge.
The judge said, "You've been brought here for drinking."
The drunk said, "OK, let's get started!"

⬤

A man and a woman who have never met before find themselves in the same sleeping carriage on a train. After the initial embarrassment they both manage to get to sleep, the woman on the top bunk, the man on the lower. In the middle of the night the woman leans over and says, "I'm sorry to bother you but I'm awfully cold and I was wondering if you could possibly pass me another blanket."
The man leans out and with a glint in his eye says, "I've got a better idea - let's pretend we're married."
"Why not!" giggles the woman.
"Good," he replies. "Get your own damn blanket."

⬤

Give a man a fish and he will eat for a day. Teach a man how to fish and he'll sit in a boat and drink beer all day.

George set out on a very windy night to see his friend Sam, who was sick in bed. Hours later, George dragged his weary body into Sam's house, and collapsed on the sofa, exhausted. "I'll tell you," George said, when he had caught his breath, "it was just brutal. For every step I took forward, I fell back two."

"So how did you ever make it over here?" Sam asked.

"Well," George replied, "after a while I decided to give up, so I turned around and headed for home."

A peevish golfer, on his way to a record bad score, began to berate his caddie.

"You must be the worst caddie in the world," he railed.

"That," said the caddie, "would be too much of a coincidence, sir."

A group of attorneys had to measure the height of a flagpole for evidence to support a lawsuit. They went out to the flagpole with ladders and a tape measure. They proceed to fall off the ladders and drop the tape measure — the whole thing was just a mess. An engineer comes along and sees what they're trying to do. He walks over, pulls the flagpole out of the ground, lays it flat, measures it from end to end, gives the measurements to one of the attorneys and walks away. After the engineer has gone, one attorney turns to another and laughs. "Isn't that just like an engineer. We're looking for the height, and he gives us the length."

A pregnant woman has an accident and falls into a coma. When she wakes up, she sees she's no longer pregnant and she asks the doctor about her baby.

The doctor replies, "You've had twins! A boy and a girl. Your brother came in and named them."

The woman thinks to herself, "No, not my brother, he's an idiot!"

She asks the doctor, "Well, what's the girl's name?"

"Denise."

"Wow, that's not a bad name, I like it! What's the boy's name"

"Denephew."

Two elderly ladies were discussing their husbands over tea.

"I do wish that my Elmer would stop biting his nails. He makes me terribly nervous."

"My Billy used to do the same thing," the older woman replied. "But I broke him of the habit."

"How?"

"I hid his teeth."

A gang of robbers broke into a lawyers' club by mistake. The old legal lions gave them the fight of their lives. The gang was very happy to escape.

"It ain't so bad," one crook noted. "We got out with $25 between us."

"I warned you to stay clear of lawyers!" the boss screamed. "We had over $100 when we broke in!"

Patient: Doctor, my wife thinks I'm crazy because I like sausages.
Psychiatrist: Nonsense! I like sausages too.
Patient: Good, you should come see my collection.

●

Man: So, wanna go back to my place?
Woman: Well, I don't know. Will two people fit under a rock?

●

A carpet layer had just finished fitting a carpet for a woman. He stepped out for a smoke, only to realize he'd lost his cigarettes. In the middle of the room, under the carpet, was a bump. No sense pulling up the entire carpet for one pack of smokes, he said to himself. He proceeded to get out his hammer and flattened the hump.

As he was cleaning up, the woman came in. "Here," she said, handing him his pack of cigarettes. "I found them in the hallway. Have you seen anything of my pet tortoise?"

A man was in no shape to drive, so he wisely left his car parked and walked home. As he was walking unsteadily along, he was stopped by a policeman.

"What are you doing out here at 2 am?" said the officer.

"I'm going to a lecture," the man said.

"And who is going to give a lecture at this hour?" the policeman asked.

"My wife," said the man.

A prince who has been turned into a frog is wandering in the forest bemoaning the fact that he never meets any princesses when he meets a wizard. "Cheer up," says the wizard, "You'll soon meet a beautiful young girl who will want to know all about you."

"When?" asks the frog.

"Next week in her biology class."

We used to play spin the bottle when I was a kid. A girl would spin the bottle, and if the bottle pointed to you when it stopped, the girl could either kiss you or give you a penny. By the time I was 14, I owned my own home.

An anxious wife is watching her husband fish in a bucket of water in the middle of the living room.

"I'd take him to a psychiatrist," she says. "But we need the fish."

A man tried to sell his neighbor a new dog. "This is a talking dog," he said. "And you can have him for $10."

The neighbor said, "Who do you think you're kidding with this talking-dog stuff? There's no such animal."

Suddenly the dog looked up with tears in his eyes. "Please buy me, sir," he pleaded. "This man is cruel. He never buys me a meal, never bathes me, never takes me for a walk. And I used to be the richest trick dog in the world. I performed before kings. I was in the army and was decorated ten times."

"Hey!" said the neighbor. "He can talk. Why do you want to sell him for just $10?"

"Because," said the seller, "I'm sick of his lies."

❍

Two hydrogen atoms walk into a bar.
One says, "I think I've lost an electron."
The other says "Are you sure?"
The first says, "Yes, I'm positive."

❍

Three wise blind elephants were discussing what humans are like. They couldn't agree so they decided to find out what humans are like by direct experience. They set off through the jungle until they heard the sound of voices. Gradually they drew nearer and nearer. Finally, the first wise blind elephant felt a human and declared, "Humans are flat."

The other wise blind elephants, after feeling the human, agreed.

A film crew was on location deep in the desert. One day an old Indian went up to the director and said, "Tomorrow rain." The next day it rained. A week later, the Indian went up to the director and said, "Tomorrow storm." The next day there was a hailstorm. "This Indian is incredible," said the director. He told his secretary to hire the Indian to predict the weather. However, after several successful predictions, the old Indian didn't show up for two weeks.

Finally the director sent for him. "I have to shoot a big scene tomorrow," said the director, "and I'm depending on you. What will the weather be like?"

The Indian shrugged his shoulders. "Don't know," he said. "Radio is broken."

A husband is advised by a psychiatrist to assert himself, "You don't have to let your wife henpeck you. Go home and show her you're the boss."

The husband takes the doctor's advice. He rushes home, slams the door, shakes his fist in his wife's face, and growls, "From now on, you're taking orders from me. I want my supper right now, and when you get it on the table, go upstairs, and lay out my best clothes. Tonight, I'm going out with the boys, and you are going to stay at home where you belong. And another thing, guess who's going to comb my hair, give me a shave, and straighten my tie?"

His wife says calmly, "The undertaker."

A man hasn't been feeling well, so he goes to his doctor for a complete checkup. Afterward, the doctor comes out with the results.

"I'm afraid I have some very bad news," the doctor says. "You're dying, and you don't have much time left."

"Oh, that's terrible!" says the man. "Give it to me straight, Doc. How long have I got?"

"Ten," the doctor says sadly.

"Ten?" the man asks. "Ten what? Months? Weeks? What?!"

"Nine...""

I noticed my husband standing on the bathroom scale, sucking in his stomach. Thinking he was trying to weigh less with this maneuver, I commented, "I don't think that is going to help."

"Sure it does," he said. "It's the only way I can see the numbers!"

After completing his examination, the doctor took the patient's husband aside. "I don't like the look of your wife at all."
"Me neither, Doc," said the husband. "But she's a good cook and the kids seem to like her."

○

After living in a remote wilderness all his life, an old codger decided it was time to visit the big city. In one of the shops he picks up a mirror and looks into it. Not knowing what it was, he remarked, "How about that! Here's a picture of my daddy."
He bought the 'picture', but on the way home he remembered his wife, Lizzy, didn't like his father. So he hung it in the barn, and every morning before leaving for the fields, he would go there and look at it.
Lizzy began to get suspicious of these trips to the barn. One day after her husband left, she searched the barn and found the mirror. As she looked into the glass, she fumed, "So that's the old gal he's runnin' after."

○

Biff: What's the name of your ranch?
Cliff: The Dun Rovin' Free As An Eagle Cattle Ranch.
Biff: How many head of cattle do you have?
Cliff: Four.
Biff: How come?
Cliff: They were the only ones to survive the branding.

One fellow sent to prison wasn't worried at all about serving his full term. When asked why, he said his wife had never let him finish a sentence the whole time they'd been married.

A young couple invited their vicar for Sunday dinner. While they were in the kitchen preparing the meal, the priest asked their son what they were having. "Goat," the little boy replied. "Goat?" asked the startled man of the cloth, "Are you sure about that?"
"Yep," said the youngster. "I heard Dad say to Mom, 'Might as well have the old goat for dinner today as any other day.'"

The length of a minute depends on which side of a bathroom door you're standing on.

A kangaroo kept getting out of his enclosure at the zoo. After recapturing the kangaroo, the zookeeper put up a ten-foot fence. Again the kangaroo was out the next morning, roaming around the zoo. So the fence was extended to twenty feet. But again the kangaroo was out the next morning. Frustrated zoo officials built a fence forty feet high.
A camel in the next enclosure asked the kangaroo, "How much higher do you think they'll go?"
The kangaroo said, "Who knows? — unless somebody starts locking the gate!"

A blonde is terribly overweight, so her doctor put her on a diet. "I want you to eat regularly for two days, then skip a day, and repeat this procedure for two weeks. The next time I see you, you'll have lost at least five pounds." When the blonde returned, she shocked the doctor by having lost nearly 20 pounds. "Why, that's amazing!" the doctor said, "Did you follow my instructions?"

The blonde nodded, "I'll tell you though, I thought I was going to drop dead the third day."

"From hunger, you mean?" asked the doctor.

"No, from skipping."

A man put a coin in a vending machine and watched helplessly while the cup failed to appear. One nozzle sent coffee down the drain while another poured cream after it.

"Now that's real automation!" he exclaimed. "It even drinks for you!"

If you love something, set it free.

If it comes back, it will always be yours.

If it doesn't come back, it was never yours to begin with.

But, if it just sits in your living room, makes a mess, eats your food, uses your telephone, takes your money, and doesn't appear to realize that you had set it free,

you either married it or gave birth to it.

Teacher: Johnny, give me a sentence starting with 'I'
Little Johnny: I is...
Teacher: No, Little Johnny. Always say 'I am.'
Little Johnny: All right. I am the ninth letter of the alphabet.

Deep within a forest a little turtle began to climb a tree. After hours of effort he reached the top, jumped into the air frantically waving his front legs and crashed to the ground. After recovering, he slowly climbed the tree again, jumped, and fell to the ground. The turtle tried again and again while a couple of birds sitting on a branch watched his sad efforts. Finally, the female bird turned to her mate.
"Dear," she chirped, "I think it's time to tell him he's adopted."

Why won't sharks attack lawyers?
Professional courtesy.

Why does an elephant never forget?
What has he got to remember?

Why did the Maharishi refuse anesthetic when he had his
tooth pulled?
He wanted to transcend dental medication.

What's covered in cellophane and climbs up and down a rope?
The lunchpack of Notre Dame.

How many witches does it take to change a light bulb?
Into what?

How many existentialists does it take to screw in a light bulb?
Two: one to screw it in and one to observe how the light bulb
itself symbolizes a single incandescent beacon of subjective
reality in a netherworld of endless absurdity reaching out
toward a cosmos of nothingness.

What would get a man to put down the toilet seat?
A sex-change operation.

What should you give a man who has everything?
Penicillin

What's the difference between a lawyer and a herd of buffalo?
The lawyer charges more.

Why were the cannibals sick after eating the missionary?
You can't keep a good man down.

What's the difference between a blonde and a shopping trolley?
A shopping trolley has a mind of its own.

What's the difference between a bad golfer and a bad skydiver?
A bad golfer goes WHACK! "Oh no!" A bad skydiver goes "Oh
no!" WHACK!

What's the most common cause of hearing loss amongst men?
A woman saying she wants to talk about their relationship.

Why do men chase women that they have no intention
of marrying?
For the same reason dogs chase cars that they have no
intention of driving.

A dog goes into a butcher's shop with a note asking for three pounds of his best mince and a $10 note in a basket. The butcher goes to the window and reaches for the dried up stuff that's been sitting out all day. The dog growls at him. The butcher turns around and, glaring at the pup, gets the best mince from the fridge. He weighs out about two and a half pounds. "Hmm, a bit shy. Who'll know?" Again, the dog growls menacingly. The butcher throws on a generous half pound, wraps it up, drops it in the basket, and drops in change from $5. The dog threatens to chew him off at the ankles. Another $5 note goes in the basket. The butcher is impressed and decides to follow the dog home. After crossing the town the dog enters a building, pushes the lift button, enters the lift, and then pushes the button for the 12th floor. The dog walks down the corridor and smartly bangs the basket on the door. The door opens, and the dog's owner starts screaming angrily at the dog.

"Hey, what are you doing? That's an amazing dog you've got there," comments the butcher.

"He's a stupid dog - that's the third time this week he's forgotten his key."

"May I take your order?" the waiter asked.

"Yes. I'm just wondering, how do you prepare your chickens?"

"Nothing special sir," he replied. "We just tell them straight out that they're going to die."

A man rushed into the doctor's office and shouted, "Doctor! I think I'm shrinking!"
The doctor calmly responded, "Now, settle down, sir. You'll just have to be a little patient."

●

He: This coffee isn't fit for a pig!
She: No problem, I'll get you some that is.

●

A father brought his son into the doctor because the boy had a toy car shoved up his nose. All the while the doctor was trying to remove the car, the father kept saying, "I don't know how he did it!" Finally the doctor removed the car, and the father and son left.
A few hours later, the father came back with the same toy car shoved up his nose. He told the doctor, "I know how he did it!"

A doctor and a lawyer were talking at a party. Their conversation was constantly interrupted by people describing their ailments and asking the doctor for free medical advice. After an hour of this, the exasperated doctor asked the lawyer, "What do you do to stop people from asking you for legal advice when you're out of the office?"

"I give it to them," replied the lawyer, "and then I send them a bill."

The doctor thought this a good idea and opened his office early the next day to give himself time to write out some invoices. When he arrived, he found a bill from the lawyer.

◐

A prisoner in jail received a letter from his wife:

"I have decided to plant some lettuce in the back garden. When is the best time to plant it?"

The prisoner, knowing that the prison guards read all the mail, replied in a letter:

"Dear Wife, whatever you do, DO NOT touch the back garden! That is where I hid all the gold."

A week or so later, he received another letter from his wife:

"You wouldn't believe what happened. Some men came with shovels to the house, and dug up the whole back garden."

The prisoner wrote another letter:

"Dear Wife, NOW is the best time to plant the lettuce!"

A young man saw an elderly couple sitting down to lunch in a restaurant. He noticed that they had ordered one meal, and an extra cup. As he watched, the gentleman carefully divided the steak in half, then counted out the chips, one for him, one for her, until each had half of them. Then he poured half of the soft drink into the extra cup and set that in front of his wife. The old man then began to eat, and his wife sat watching, with her hands folded in her lap.

The young man decided to ask if they would allow him to purchase another meal for them so that they didn't have to split theirs. The old gentleman said, "Oh, no. We've been married 50 years, and everything has always been and will always be shared, 50/50." The young man then asked the wife if she was going to eat, and she replied,

"Not yet. It's his turn with the teeth."

Hypochondriac: Doctor, if I give up drinking and smoking, cut out fat from my diet, avoid gambling, driving fast cars and chasing women, will I live to be 100?

Doctor: No, but it'll seem like it.

Two little boys were talking in Hollywood. "How are you getting on with your new dad?" one asked.

"Oh, all right, I suppose," said the other. "Have you met him?"

"Of course," said the first boy. "We had him last year."

Men make the larger sacrifice when they get married. They generally give up doing their cleaning, their cooking, their shopping and their laundry.

While the brokers were busily calling potential customers to drum up business, the president of the firm stopped to eavesdrop on a new employee. He listened as the young man talked eight consecutive contacts into moving their stock portfolios to him.

The boss approached the young man and said, "I've been listening in, and I must say I'm impressed with your ability. Where did you learn so much about talking to investors?"

"Yale, sir," the young man answered.

Impressed, the boss said, "Oh, that's fine, just fine. And what's your name?"

"Yohn Yackson," he replied.

While proudly showing off his new apartment to friends, a student led the way into the den. "What's the big brass gong and hammer for?" one of his friends asked.

"That's the talking clock," the man replied, and his friend wanted to know how it worked.

"Watch," the man said, then proceeded to give the gong an ear-shattering pound with the hammer, producing a loud BONG! Suddenly someone screamed from the other side of the wall, "KEEP IT DOWN YOU IDIOT! It's two o'clock in the morning!"

A man walked into a lawyer's office and inquired about the lawyer's rates.

"$50 for three questions," replied the lawyer.

"Isn't that awfully steep?" asked the man.

"Yes," the lawyer replied, "and what was your third question?"

It isn't necessary for a politician to fool all the people all the time. A majority on election day is enough.

A young man hired by a supermarket reported for his first day of work. The manager greeted him with a warm handshake and a smile, gave him a broom and said, "Your first job will be to sweep the floor."

"But I'm a graduate," the young man replied indignantly.

"Oh, I'm sorry. I didn't know that," said the manager. "Here, give me the broom - I'll show you how."

A man approached an idiot in a village he was visiting.
".What's the quickest way to London?"
The idiot scratched his head.
"Are you walking or driving?" he asked the stranger.
"I'm driving."
"That's the quickest way."

◊

Three idiots are given a simple test during a job interview. The interviewer says to the first idiot, "What is three times three?"
"274," was his reply.
The interviewer says to the second idiot, "It's your turn. What is three times three?"
"Tuesday," replies the second idiot.
The interviewer says to the third idiot, "Okay, your turn. What's three times three?"
"Nine," says the third idiot.
"That's great!" says the interviewer. "How did you get that?"
"Simple," says the third idiot. "I just subtracted 274 from Tuesday."

◊

An insurance agent was teaching his wife to drive when the brakes suddenly failed going down a steep hill.
"I can't stop!" she shrilled. "What should I do?"
"Brace yourself, "advised her husband, "and try to hit something cheap."

Three aspiring psychiatrists from various colleges were attending their first class on emotional extremes.

"Just to establish some parameters," said the professor, to the student from New York, "What is the opposite of joy?"

"Sadness," said the student.

"And the opposite of depression?" he asked of the young lady from Harvard.

"Elation."

"And you sir," he said to the young man from Texas, "how about the opposite of woe?"

The Texan replied, "Sir, I believe that would be giddy-up."

A married man left work early one Friday afternoon. Instead of going home, he squandered the weekend and his paycheck partying with his friends, never calling his wife. When he finally returned home on Sunday night, he ran into a furious wife. After a couple of hours of yelling and screaming, his wife asked, "How would you like it if you didn't see me for a couple of days?"

He responded, "That would suit me just fine."

So, Monday went by, and the man didn't see his wife. Tuesday and Wednesday came and went with the same result. On Thursday, the swelling went down enough so that he could see her a little, just out of the corner of his left eye.

What's the best way to go gambling in Las Vegas and come back with a small fortune?
Go with a large fortune.

◊

Why are men like horoscopes?
They always tell you what to do and they are usually wrong.

◊

What does it mean when the man of the house suddenly showers you with affection, tenderness and sympathy?
You're in the wrong house.

◊

Did you hear about the blonde who stood in front of the mirror with her eyes closed?
She wanted to see what she looked like asleep.

◊

What do you call a man who's been buried for 2000 years?
Pete.

◊

What's the difference between a man and a parrot?
You can teach a parrot to say, "No".

◊

How are men like a used car?
Both are easy to get, cheap, and unreliable.

◊

What do you get if you cross a skeleton with a dog?
An animal that buries itself.

Why do men come home drunk and leave their clothes on the floor?
Because they are still wearing them.

How many men does it take to wallpaper a bathroom?
Three, if you slice them very thinly.

What is the difference between a new husband and a new dog?
After a year, the dog is still excited to see you.

What do you call a man with a shovel in his head?
Doug.

What do you get if you cross an elephant with a bottle of whisky?
Trunk and disorderly.

A pickpocket was up in court for a series of petty crimes. The judge said "Mr Banks you are hereby fined $100."
The lawyer stood up and said "Your honor, my client only has $75 on him at this time, but if you'd allow him a few minutes in the crowd..."

Men are like animals — messy, insensitive and potentially violent.
But they make great pets.

Two men were stopped by a TV newswoman doing street interviews about the upcoming election. "I'm not voting for any of the candidates," the first man said. "I don't know any of them."
"I feel the same way," the second man said. "Only I know them all."

The only time a woman really succeeds in changing a man is when he's a baby.

A fellow took his talking dog to a show business talent agent, and the dog told six or eight familiar old jokes, including a couple with French and English accents.
"What do you think?" the dog's owner asked the agent. "We're gonna make a fortune, right?"
"Well," the agent replied, "his delivery's all right, but his material's weak."

A dejected politician trudges home after the polls close.
"So, how many votes did you get?" asked his wife.
"Two," he responds.
She slaps him hard across the face.
"What was that for?" he asks.
"You have a mistress, now, do you?"

A little girl asks a little boy, "Hey Tommy, do you want to play house?"
He says, "Sure! What do you want me to do?"
The girl replies, "I want you to communicate your feelings."
"Communicate my feelings?" said a bewildered Tommy. "I have no idea what that means."
The little girl smirks and says, "Perfect. You can be the husband."

A lawyer and an engineer were fishing in the Caribbean. The lawyer said, "I'm here because my house burned down and everything I owned was destroyed by the fire. The insurance company paid for everything."
"That's quite a coincidence," said the engineer, "I'm here because my house and all my belongings were destroyed by a flood, and my insurance company also paid for everything."
The lawyer looked somewhat confused. "How do you start a flood?" he asked.

Fresh out of business school, a young man answered an ad for an accountant. He was interviewed by a very nervous man who ran a small business that he had started himself.

"I need someone with an accounting degree," the man said. "But mainly, I'm looking for someone to do my worrying for me."

"Excuse me?" the accountant said.

"I worry about a lot of things," the man said. "But I don't want to have to worry about money. Your job will be to take all the money worries off my back."

"I see," the accountant said. "And how much does the job pay?"

"I'll start you at $60,000."

"$60,000!" the accountant exclaimed. "How can such a small business afford a sum like that?"

""That," the owner said, "is your first worry."

◐

A mother was reading her eight-year-old one of her favorite fairy tales. "Mommy," asked the little girl, "do all fairy tales begin with 'Once Upon a Time?'"

"No, dearest," replied her mom, "sometimes they start with 'Darling, I have to work a little late at the office tonight.'"

◐

Before marriage a man will lay awake all night thinking about something you said.

After marriage, he'll fall asleep before you finish saying it.

Adam and Eve had an ideal marriage. He didn't have to hear about all the men she could have married, and she didn't have to hear about the way his mother cooked.

◊

A little boy had just got home from an outing with his dad.
"How was the zoo?" asked his mom.
"It was great," he said "Dad got really excited when one of the animals won by a neck at 33-1."

◊

A very dirty little fellow came in from playing in the garden and asked his mother, "Who am I?"
Ready to play the game she said, "I don't know! Who are you?"
"WOW!" cried the child. "Mrs Johnson was right! She said I was so dirty, my own mother wouldn't recognize me!"

If at first you don't succeed, skydiving isn't for you.

"Daddy, where did I come from?" the seven-year-old asked. It was a moment for which her parents had carefully prepared. They took her into the living room, got out the encyclopedia and several other books, and explained all they thought she should know about sexual attraction, affection, love, and reproduction. Then they both sat back and smiled contentedly.
"Does that answer your question?" her father asked.
"Not really," the little girl said. "Jane said she came from Birmingham. I want to know where I came from."

Early one morning, a mother went to her sleeping son and woke him up.
"Wake up, son. It's time to go to school."
"I don't want to go to school."
"Why not?"
"All the children hate me. All the teachers hate me."
"Oh! that's no reason. Come on, you have to go to school,"
"Give me two good reasons why I should go to school?"
"One, you are fifty-two years old. Two, you are the headmaster of the school."

I married Miss Right. I just didn't know her first name was Always.

A honeymoon couple is in the Watergate Hotel in Washington.
The bride is concerned "What if the place is still bugged?"
The groom says, "I'll look for a bug."
He looks behind the drapes, behind the pictures, under the
carpet "AHA!" Under the carpet was a disc with four screws. He
gets his Swiss army knife, unscrews the screws, throws them
and the disc out the window.
The next morning, the hotel manager asks the newlyweds
"How was your room? How was the service? How was your stay
at the Watergate Hotel?"
The groom says, "Why are you asking us all of these questions?"
The hotel manager says, "Well, the room under you complained
that the chandelier fell on them!"

Men are like bike helmets.
They are good in emergencies, but otherwise they just
look silly.

Two dogs were walking down the street.
One dog says to the other, "Wait here a minute, I'll be right
back." He walks across the street and sniffs a fire hydrant for
about a minute, then walks back across the street.
The other dog asks, "What was that about?"
The first dog says, "Oh, I was just checking my messages."

A man went to heaven and found St Peter at the door.
"We have a very long list and we are choosy. Have you done a good deed recently?" asked St Peter.
"Oh yes. I was coming back from work at night and I saw some men attacking a poor old woman. I approached the one who seemed their leader and gave him a punch straight in his face. The others surrounded me. I started shouting at them to leave the old woman because otherwise I would have given them a lesson that they will long remember."
St. Peter was impressed: "Well done, when did that happen?"
"Five minutes ago."

The mother of a problem child was advised by a psychiatrist, "You are far too upset and worried about your son. I suggest you take tranquilizers regularly."
On her next visit the psychiatrist asked, "Have the tranquilizers calmed you down?"
"Yes," the mother answered.
"And how is your son now?" he asked.
"Who cares?" she replied.

A beggar walked up to a well-dressed woman out shopping and said, "I haven't eaten anything in four days."
She looked at him and said, "I wish I had your willpower."

A man spoke frantically into the phone: "She's pregnant, in labor and her contractions are only two minutes apart!"

"Is this her first child?" asked the doctor.

"NO, YOU IDIOT" the man shouted, "This is her husband!"

Bob, an experienced skydiver, was getting ready for a jump one day when he spotted another man all kitted out to skydive wearing dark glasses, carrying a white cane and holding a guide dog by an extremely long leash.

Shocked that the blind man was also going to jump, Bob struck up a conversation, expressing his admiration for the man's courage. Then, curious, he asked, "How do you know when the ground is getting close?"

"Easy," replied the blind man. "The leash goes slack."

A father was trying to teach his young son the evils of alcohol. He put one worm in a glass of water and another worm in a glass of whiskey. The worm in the water lived, while the one in the whiskey curled up and died.

"All right, son," asked the father, "what does that show you?"

"Well, Dad, it shows that if you drink alcohol, you will not have worms."

A couple of hunters are out stalking in the woods when one of them falls to the ground.

He doesn't seem to be breathing and his eyes are rolled back in his head. The other hunter whips out his mobile phone and calls the emergency services. He gasps to the operator, "My friend is dead! What can I do?"

The operator, in a calm soothing voice says, "Just take it easy. I can help. First, let's make sure he's dead..."

There is a silence, then a shot is heard. The hunter says, "OK, now what?"

An airline recently introduced a special half fare for wives who accompanied their husbands on business trips.

Expecting valuable testimonials, the PR department sent out letters to all the wives of businessmen who had used the special rates, asking how they enjoyed their trip.

Letters are still pouring in asking, "What trip?"

Just think, if it weren't for marriage, men would go through life thinking they had no faults at all.

A blonde went to buy a television but the salesperson told her, "I'm sorry but we don't sell anything to blondes, that's a strict policy." She went away and returned a week later, but none of the staff would sell her a television because she was a blonde. At home she dyed her hair brown as a disguise, returned once more to the shop and asked the salesperson, "Can I buy that television?"

The salesperson reiterated, "I'm sorry but we don't sell anything to blondes — that's a strict policy."

The blonde, impressed, asked, "But how do you know that I am a blonde?"

The salesperson replied, "Because only a blonde would confuse a microwave and a television."

This couple are getting on in years, so the husband thinks, "I'll buy my wife a cemetery plot for her birthday." Well, you can imagine her disappointment. The next year, her birthday rolls around again and he doesn't get her anything. She says, "Why didn't you get me a birthday present?"

He says, "You didn't use what I got you last year!"

Two Eskimos sitting in a kayak were chilly, but when they lit a fire in the craft, it sank, proving once again that you can't have your kayak and heat it, too.

A passenger plane on a cross-country trip runs into a terrible storm. The plane gets pounded by rain, hail, wind and lightning. The passengers are sure the plane is going to crash and that they are all going to die. At the height of the storm, a young woman jumps up and exclaims, "I can't take this anymore! I can't just sit here and die like an animal, strapped into a chair. If I am going to die, let me at least die feeling like a woman. Is there anyone here man enough to make me feel like a woman?"

A man at the back of the plane stands up and hands her his shirt. "Here," he says, "Iron this."

An attractive young woman, chaperoned by an ugly old crone, entered the doctor's office.

"We have come for an examination," said the young woman.

"All right," said the doctor. "Go behind that curtain and take your clothes off."

"No, not me," said the girl. "It's my old aunt here."

"Very well," said the doctor. "Madam, stick out your tongue."

A man is giving a speech at a meeting. He gets a bit carried away and talks for two hours. Finally, he realizes what he is doing and says, "I'm sorry I talked so long. I left my watch at home."

A voice from the back of the room calls out, "There's a calendar behind you."

A man inserted an ad in the newspaper: "Wife wanted." Next day he received a 100 letters. They all said the same thing: "You can have mine."

◐

An out-of-towner drove his car into a ditch in a desolated area. Luckily, a local farmer came to help with his big strong horse named Buddy. He hitched Buddy up to the car and yelled, "Pull, Nellie, pull!" Buddy didn't move. Then the farmer hollered, "Pull, Buster, pull!" Buddy didn't respond. Once more the farmer commanded, "Pull, Coco, pull!" Nothing. Then the farmer nonchalantly said, "Pull, Buddy, pull!" And the horse easily dragged the car out of the ditch. The motorist was most appreciative and very curious. He asked the farmer why he called his horse by the wrong name three times. The farmer said, "Oh, Buddy is blind and if he thought he was the only one pulling, he wouldn't even try!"

A man is walking home alone late one night when he hears a BUMP... BUMP... BUMP... behind him.

Walking faster he looks back, and makes out the image of an upright coffin banging its way down the middle of the street towards him. BUMP... BUMP... BUMP...

Terrified, the man begins to run towards his home, the coffin bouncing quickly behind him... BUMP... BUMP.... BUMP... He runs up to his door, fumbles with his keys, opens the door, rushes in, slams and locks the door behind him, with the coffin banging against the door. Rushing upstairs to the bathroom, the man locks himself in. His heart is pounding; his head is reeling; his breath is coming in sobbing gasps. With a loud CRASH the coffin breaks down the door, bumping towards him. The man screams and reaches for something, anything, but all he can find is a bottle of cough syrup!

Desperate, he throws the cough syrup at the coffin.

The coffin stops.

A man takes his Rottweiler to the vet. "My dog's cross-eyed — is there anything you can do for him?"

"Well," says the vet, "let's have a look at him." So he picks the dog up and examines his eyes, then checks his teeth. Finally, he says "I'm going to have to put him down."

"What? Because he's cross-eyed?"

"No, because he's really heavy."

A barber gave a haircut to a priest one day. The priest tried to pay for the haircut but the barber refused saying "You do God's work." The next morning the barber found a dozen bibles at the door to his shop.

A doctor came to the barber for a haircut, and again the barber refused payment saying "You heal the public." The next morning the barber found a box of medicine at the door to his shop.

A lawyer came to the barber for a haircut, and again the barber refused payment saying "You serve the justice system." The next morning the barber found a dozen lawyers waiting for a haircut.

◐

I married my wife for her looks, but not the ones she's been giving me lately!

◐

Knock! Knock!
Who's there?
Olive.
Olive who?
Olive across the road.

◐

Late one night in London a mugger jumped a well-dressed man and held a gun to his ribs.
"Give me your money!" he demanded.
The man stiffened, but said indignantly, "You can't do this to me, I'm a Member of Parliament."
"In that case," replied the robber, "give me my money!"

What happened to the hyena who swallowed an Oxo cube?
He made a laughing stock of himself.

What did the cannibal return home with one leg missing?
He'd been on a self-catering holiday.

What's the difference between men and pigs?
Pigs don't get drunk and turn into men.

What did the grape do when it was stepped on?
It let out a little wine.

What do you call a woman who has one leg shorter than the other?
Eileen.

What did the hat say to the scarf?
You hang around while I go on a head.

What happens if you don't pay the exorcist?
You get repossessed.

What happened when the policeman caught a boy drinking battery acid and another eating fireworks?
He charged one and let the other off.

Why did the bees go on strike?
They wanted more honey and fewer flowers.

●

What's the definition of experience?
Something you don't get until just after you need it.

●

What do you call a boomerang that doesn't come back?
A stick.

●

Why do oysters never give money to charity?
Because they're shellfish.

●

Why do black widow spiders eat their males after mating?
To stop them from snoring.

●

Why did Robin Hood only rob the rich?
The poor didn't have anything worth stealing.

Confucius say: Man who run in front of car get tired, man who run behind car get exhausted.

A taxi driver driving a Mercedes-Benz picked up a rather simple-looking fellow at the airport one day.
When the gentleman got in and they started on their way he inquired what the emblem on the front was for. The driver, fancying himself a bit of a wag, replied "That's for lining it up at people so you can run them down."
A couple of minutes later the driver had to swerve violently to avoid an elderly woman who stepped out into the road. He just missed her and then heard a loud bang. He looked over at the passenger who was hanging out of the car with the door wide open, "I thought you were going to miss there for a minute!"

A man and a little boy entered a barbershop together. After the man received the full treatment – shave, shampoo, manicure, haircut, etc – he placed the boy in the chair. "I'm going to buy a paper," he said. "I'll be back in a few minutes." When the boy's haircut was completed and the man still hadn't returned, the barber said, "Looks like your daddy's forgotten all about you." "That wasn't my daddy," said the boy. "He just walked up, took me by the hand and said, 'Come on, son, we're gonna get a free haircut!'"

A new prisoner is placed in his cell with a cellmate. Before long it is time for 'lights out' and the dark cellblock becomes nearly silent. Eventually a voice from across the cellblock cries out "twenty-two!" and everyone breaks out into loud and prolonged laughter. A little while later another voice calls out "forty-one!" and again the entire cellblock enjoys a hearty laugh. The new prisoner is confused and asks his cellmate what this is all about. The cellmate replies that they have been in prison so long that rather than tell the same jokes over and over, they have assigned numbers to them as a more efficient way to tell jokes. The new prisoner asks if he could give it a try. His cellmate says "Sure, why not tell number eighteen!"
The new prisoner shouts out "eighteen!" No response whatsoever. The new prisoner is confused and asks his cellmate what went wrong.
The cellmate replies, "Some people just don't know how to tell a joke!"

Two boll weevils grew up in the Deep South. One went to Hollywood and became a famous actor. The other stayed behind in the cotton fields and never amounted to much. The second one, naturally, became known as the lesser of two weevils.

If you want your wife to listen and pay undivided attention to every word you say, talk in your sleep.

The efficiency expert concluded his lecture with a note of caution, "You don't want to try these techniques at home."

"Why not?" asked someone from the back of the audience.

"I watched my wife's routine at breakfast for years, "the expert explained. "She made lots of trips to the refrigerator, cooker, table and kitchen cabinets, often carrying just a single item at a time.

'Darling,' I suggested, 'Why don't you try carrying several things at once?'"

The voice from the back asked, "Did it save time?"

The expert replied, "Actually, yes. It used to take her 20 minutes to get breakfast ready. Now I do it in seven."

🥚

A golfer stood over his tee shot for what seemed an eternity. He was driving his partner mad, as he looked up, looked down, measured the distance, calculated the wind direction and speed. Finally, his exasperated partner said, "What's taking so long? Just hit the ball!"

The man answers, "My wife's up there watching me from the clubhouse. I want to make this a perfect shot."

His partner mumbled, "Forget it, man, you'll never hit her from here!"

🥚

Good judgement comes from bad experience, and a lot of that comes from bad judgement.

A man walked into a bar and sat down beside a woman. Suddenly her glass eye popped out and he caught it. She thanked him and asked him if he would join her for breakfast the next day. He agreed and got her address. The next day he went to her house and had a lovely breakfast. He asked, "Do you treat all men like this?"

She smiled and said, "Just the ones who catch my eye."

An elderly man, who had had a little too much to drink, was walking along the road. A big truck came along and knocked him down. The driver stopped, got out and yelled at the old man "Hey watch out."

The old man look at the driver and asked, "Why? You gonna back up?"

The local priest was visiting old Mrs Jones to comfort her after the recent loss of her husband. Sitting on the sofa, the priest eyed a dish of peanuts on the coffee table. He took a few of the peanuts and began to eat them. After ten minutes he noticed that he had eaten nearly all the peanuts. "Why Mrs Jones," he said, "It appears that I have eaten almost all your peanuts." "Don't worry Father," replied Mrs Jones "Now that I've lost all my teeth I only get to suck the chocolate off!"

A man realizes he needs to buy a hearing aid, but he is unwilling to spend much money.
"How much do they cost?" he asks the salesman.
"That depends," says the salesman. "They range from $2 to $2,000."
"Let's see the $2 model," the customer says.
The salesman puts the device around the man's neck. "You just stick this button in your ear and run this little string down to your pocket," he says.
"How does it work?" the customer asks.
"For $2, it doesn't work," the salesman replies. "But when people see it on you, they'll talk louder."

What did the lawyer name his daughter?
Sue.
And his son?
Bill.

Drover: You know, that cow of mine has as much sense as I do.
Luke: Well, don't tell anybody. You might want to sell her
one day.

Two rabbits were being chased by a pack of wolves. The wolves
chased the rabbits into a thicket. After a few minutes, one
rabbit turned to the other and said,
"Well, do you want to make a run for it or stay here a few days
and outnumber them?"

Adam was walking around the Garden of Eden feeling very
lonely, so God asked him, "What is wrong with you?" Adam said
he didn't have anyone to talk to. God said that He was going to
make Adam a companion and that it would be a woman. He
said, "This person will gather food for you, cook for you, and
when you discover clothing she'll wash it for you. She will
always agree with every decision you make. She will bear your
children and never ask you to get up in the middle of the night
to take care of them. She will not nag you and will always be
the first to admit she was wrong when you've had a
disagreement. She will never have a headache and will freely
give you love and passion whenever you need it."
Adam asked God, "What will a woman like this cost?"
God replied, "An arm and a leg."
Then Adam asked, "What can I get for a rib?"
The rest is history.

A 16-year-old girl bought herself a tiny bikini. She went home and put it on, then showed her mother how she looked in it. She asked, "What do you think Mom?"

Her mother replied, "I think that if I had worn that when I was your age, you'd be five years older!"

🜀

I have a dog that talks in its sleep. One day a visitor was astonished to hear the dog bellow, "My name is Christopher Columbus! I am 700 years old! I own America! I married Marilyn Monroe!"

When the visitor asked what was going on, I replied, "Don't worry about it. It's better to just let sleeping dogs lie."

🜀

A man was invited to dinner by his friend. Throughout the meal he was impressed by the way his friend preceded every request to his wife with endearing terms calling her 'Honey', 'My Love', 'Darling', 'Sweetheart', 'Pumpkin', etc. The couple had been married almost 70 years, and it seemed they were still very much in love.

While the wife was off in the kitchen, the man leaned over and said to his friend, "I think it's wonderful that, after all the years you've been married, you still call your wife those loving pet names."

The old man hung his head. "I have to tell you the truth," he said. "I forgot her name about ten years ago."

A funeral service is being held for a woman who has just passed away. At the end of the service, the pallbearers are carrying the casket out when they accidentally bump into a wall, jarring the coffin. They hear a faint moan. They open the coffin and find that the woman is actually alive! She lives for 10 more years and then dies. A ceremony is again held and, at the end of the service, the pallbearers are again carrying the casket out. As they are walking out, the husband shouts, "Watch out for the wall!"

Two friends were out on a wild drinking spree. They'd just downed the fifteenth round when one of them fell backwards off his chair and lay still on the floor.
"That's what I like about Ronnie," slurred the remaining drunk, "He always knows when to stop."

Once upon a time, an old woman had a wonderful cat. One day, a man ran over the cat accidentally with his car. So, the man went to the old woman and said, "I'm terribly sorry about your cat. I'd like to replace him."

"That so nice of you!" said the old woman, deeply touched. "So how good are you at catching mice?"

◐

Once there was a golfer whose drive landed on an anthill. Rather than move the ball, he decided to hit it where it lay. He gave a mighty swing. Clouds of dirt and sand and ants exploded from the spot. Everything but the golf ball. It sat in the same spot. So he lined up and tried another shot. Clouds of dirt and sand and ants went flying again. The golf ball didn't even wiggle. Two ants survived. One dazed ant said to the other, "Whoa! What are we going to do?"

Said the other ant, "I don't know about you, but I'm going to get on the ball."

◐

Taking his seat in his chambers, the judge faced the opposing lawyers. "So," he said, "I have been presented, by both of you, with a bribe." Both lawyers squirmed uncomfortably. "You, attorney Leon, gave me $15,000. And you, attorney Campos, gave me $10,000."

The judge reached into his pocket and pulled out a check. He handed it to Leon. "Now then, I'm returning $5,000, and we're going to decide this case solely on its merits."

A linguistics professor was lecturing to his class one day. "In English," he said, "a double negative forms a positive. In some languages though, such as Russian, a double negative is still a negative. However," he pointed out, "there is no language wherein a double positive can form a negative."

A voice from the back of the room piped up, "Yeah, right."

A middle-aged man is out to dinner with his wife to celebrate her fortieth birthday.

He says, "So what would you like, dear? A Jaguar? A diamond necklace?"

She says, "David, I want a divorce."

He says, "I wasn't planning on spending that much."

A woman goes to heaven and St Peter is showing her around and she spots loads of clocks all going at different speeds. She says to St Peter, "What are all the clocks for and why are they going at different speeds?" St Peter replies, "Everyone on Earth has a clock and every time they commit a sin the hands move."

So she asks, "Which one is my husband's clock?"

St Peter replies, "The angels are using it for a fan."

I almost had a psychic girlfriend but she left me before we met.

The early bird gets the worm, but the second mouse gets the cheese.

Two men and an idiot are lost in the desert. After days without water or food they come upon a lamp half-buried in the sand. They rub the lamp and out comes a genie. Since they all rubbed the lamp the genie grants each one a single wish.
The first man wishes he was eating dinner at the Savoy. The genie claps his hands and the man vanishes in a flash of light. The second man wishes to be transported back to his house where he knows his wife will be eagerly awaiting him. Once again the genie claps his hands and the man vanishes.
The idiot sits down and thinks about what he should wish for. Suddenly realizing he is all alone in the desert, he says: "I wish the other two were here."

A man rings up his ex-wife and, disguising his voice, asks to speak to himself.
"Sorry, he doesn't live here anymore, we're divorced!"
Next day, the man does the same thing with the same results. He does this every day for a week, and finally his ex-wife realizes who it is that keeps calling. "Look, you fool! We're divorced! Finito! End of story! When are you going to get that through your fat head?"
"Oh, I know. I just can't hear it enough!"

A magician was working on a cruise ship in the Caribbean. The audience would be different each week, so the magician performed the same tricks over and over again. There was only one problem, the captain's parrot saw the shows each week and began to understand how the magician did every trick. Once he understood he started shouting in the middle of the show, "Look, it's not the same hat." "Look, he is hiding the flowers under the table." "Hey, all the cards are the ace of spades." The magician was furious but couldn't do anything; it was, after all, the captain's parrot. One day the ship had an accident and sank. The magician found himself floating on a piece of wood in the middle of the ocean with the parrot. They stared at each other with hate, but did not utter a word. This went on for a day and another and another. After a week the parrot said, "OK, I give up. Where's the boat?"

After a long sermon the priest asked how many of his congregation were willing to forgive their enemies. About half held up their hands. Not satisfied he harangued for another twenty minutes and repeated his question. This time he received a response of about 80 percent.

Still unsatisfied, he lectured for another 15 minutes and repeated his question. With all thoughts now on Sunday dinner, all responded except one elderly lady in the rear. "Mrs Jones, are you not willing to forgive your enemies?"

"I don't have any."

"Mrs Jones, that is very unusual. How old are you?"

"93."

"Mrs Jones, please come down in front and tell the congregation how a person can live to be 93, and not have an enemy in the world."

The sweet little old lady tottered down the aisle, very slowly turned around and said, "It's easy, I just outlived all those losers!"

A Texan, a hillbilly, and a New Yorker are having dinner at a restaurant in London and the waiter tells them, "Excuse me, but we have a shortage of caviar, so disregard that item from the menu." The Texan, used to the bounty of Texas says, "What's a shortage?" The hillbilly, used to a homely diet says, "What's caviar?" and the New Yorker says, "What's 'Excuse me?'"

A hillbilly family visited New York City. One day, the father took his son into a shopping mall. They were amazed by everything they saw, especially the elevator at one end of the lobby. They had never seen anything like it.

While the boy and his father were watching in wide-eyed astonishment, an old lady in a wheelchair rolled up to the moving walls and pressed a button. The walls opened and the lady rolled between them into a small room. The walls closed and the boy and his father watched small circles of lights above the walls light up. They continued to watch the circles light up in the reverse direction. The walls opened again, and a voluptuous twenty-four-year-old woman stepped out.

The father turned to his son and said, "Go get your maw!"

◐

A young couple got married and left on their honeymoon. When they got back, the bride immediately called her mother.

"Oh, Mom," she said, "the honeymoon was wonderful! So romantic..." Suddenly, she burst out crying. "But as soon as we returned, Sam started using the most horrible language... things I had never heard before! I mean, all these awful four-letter words!"

Her mother is shocked. "Darling, tell me what he said"

Still sobbing, the bride replies, "Oh, Mom... words like DUST, WASH, IRON, COOK..."

A girl knelt in the confessional and said, "Bless me, Father, for I have sinned."
"What is it, child?"
"Father, I have committed the sin of vanity. Twice a day I gaze at myself in the mirror and tell myself how beautiful I am."
The priest turned, took a good look at the girl, and said, "My dear, I have good news. You aren't committing a sin — just a mistake."

An engineer, an accountant and a government worker were bragging about how clever their dogs are. To show off, the engineer called to his dog. "PC, do your stuff." PC trotted over to a desktop computer, grabbed the mouse in his mouth and promptly drew a circle, a square and a triangle. Everyone agreed that was pretty clever. But the accountant said his dog could do better. He called his dog and said, "Tax Break, do your stuff." Tax Break went into the kitchen and returned with a dozen biscuits. He divided them into four equal piles of three biscuits each. Everyone agreed that was good. Then the government worker called to his dog and said "Coffee Break, do your stuff." Coffee Break jumped to his feet, ate the biscuits, jumped on the computer keyboard, broke the computer assaulted the other two dogs, claimed he injured his back while doing so, filed a grievance report for unsafe working conditions, put in for compensation and went home on sick leave.

A friend hosted a dinner party for people from work, and everyone was encouraged to bring their children.
All through the sit-down dinner one co-worker's three-year-old girl stared at the man sitting across from her. The girl could hardly eat her food from staring.
The man checked his tie, felt his face for food, patted his hair in place, but nothing stopped her from staring at him. He tried his best to just ignore her but finally it was too much for him. He asked her, "Why are you staring at me?"
Everyone at the table had noticed her behavior and the table went quiet for her response.
The little girl said, "I just want to see how you drink like a fish!"

A Scotsman was out in New York wearing his tartans when a curious woman asked him if anything was worn under the kilt. "No madam," he replied. "Everything is in perfect working order."

Why did the tomato blush?
Because it saw the salad dressing.

What's the difference between a single woman and a
married woman?
A single woman comes home, takes a look at what's in the
fridge and goes to bed, a married woman comes home, takes a
look at what's in bed and goes to the fridge.

How many policeman does it take to change a light bulb?
None if it turns itself in.

Why do men prefer electric lawn mowers?
So they can find their way back to the house.

What do you get if you cross a burglar with a bunch of flowers?
Robbery with violets.

Why are men like mascara?
They run at the first sign of emotion.

What do politicians use for birth control?
Their personalities.

Why are men like placemats?
They only show up when there's food on the table.

What do you get if you pull your pants up to your neck?
A chest of drawers.

What's the definition of a transvestite?
A man that likes to eat, drink and be Mary.

How many graduate students does it take to screw in a light bulb?
Only one, but it may take him five years to do it.

Why is it dangerous to let your man's mind wander?
It's too little to be out alone.

What do you call a man with a seagull on his head?
Cliff.

Why didn't the millionaire report his stolen credit card?
The thief was spending less than his wife used to.

What's brown and sticky?
A stick.

How many stockbrokers does it take to change a light bulb?
Two. One to take out the bulb and drop it, and the other to try and sell it before it crashes (knowing that it's already burned out).

A concerned husband went to the doctor to talk about his wife. He said to the doctor, "I think my wife is deaf because she never hears me the first time and always asks me to repeat things." "Well," the doctor replied, "go home tonight, stand about 15 feet from her, and say something. If she doesn't reply, move three feet closer and say it again. Keep doing this until we get an idea about the severity of her deafness."

The husband went home and did exactly as the doctor had instructed. He started off 15 feet from his wife in the kitchen as she was chopping some vegetables.

He said, "Darling, what's for dinner?"

He heard no response. He moved three feet closer and asked again. No reply. He moved three feet closer. Still no reply. He finally got fed up and moved right behind her, about an inch away, and asked again, "Darling, what's for dinner?"

She replied, "For the fourth time, vegetable stew!"

◐

Finding one of her students making faces at others on the playground, Mrs Smith, the Sunday School teacher, smiling sweetly said, "Bobby, when I was a child I was told that if I made an ugly face, it would freeze and I would stay like that."

Bobby looked up and replied, "Well, Mrs Smith, you can't say you weren't warned."

A cowboy lay sprawled across three entire seats in the posh Amarillo cinema. When the usher came by and noticed this he whispered to the cowboy, "Sorry, sir, but you're only allowed one seat." The cowboy groaned but didn't budge. The usher became more impatient. "Sir, if you don't get up from there, I'm going to have to call the manager." The cowboy just groaned. The usher marched briskly back up the aisle. In a moment he returned with the manager. Together the two of them tried repeatedly to move the cowboy, but with no success. Finally, they summoned the police. The policeman surveyed the situation briefly then asked, "All right buddy, what's your name?"

"Sam," the cowboy moaned. "Where ya from, Sam?"
With pain in his voice Sam replied, "The balcony."

A hillbilly walked into an attorney's office wanting to file for a divorce.
The attorney asked, "May I help you?"
The hillbilly said, "Yeah, I want to get one of those dayvorces."
The attorney said, "Well, do you have any grounds?"
The hillbilly said, "Yeah, I got about 140 acres."
The attorney said, "No sir, I mean do you have a suit?"
The hillbilly said, "Yes sir, I got a suit. I wear it to church on Sundays."
The exasperated attorney said, "Well, sir, does your wife beat you up or anything?"
The hillbilly said, "No sir, we both get up about 4:30."
Finally, the attorney said, "OK, let me put it this way — WHY DO YOU WANT A DIVORCE?"
And the hillbilly replied, "Well, I can never have a meaningful conversation with her."

**mad
moose
press**